• crossing arcs •

alzheimer's, my mother, and me

• crossing arcs •

alzheimer's, my mother, and me

susan mcmaster

Black Moss Press

2009

Library and Archives Canada Cataloguing in Publication

McMaster, Susan
    Crossing arcs : Alzheimer's, my mother, and me / Susan McMaster.
Poems.
ISBN 978-0-88753-462-1
    1. Alzheimer's disease--Poetry. 2. McMaster, Susan--Family--Poetry.
3. Mothers and daughters--Poetry. I. Title.
PS8575.M33C76 2009   C811'.54   C2009-902526-4

Photographs by Marty Gervais.
Design by Karen Veryle Monck.

Published by Black Moss Press at 2450 Byng Road, Windsor, Ontario,
N8W 3E8. Canada. Black Moss books are distributed in Canada and the
U.S. by LitDistCo. All orders should be directed there.

Black Moss Press would like to acknowledge the support of the Canada
Council for the Arts and the Ontario Arts Council for their support of its
publishing program. The author thanks the Ontario Arts Council, the City
of Ottawa, and the Canada Council for the Arts for support during the
writing of this manuscript.

ONTARIO ARTS COUNCIL
CONSEIL DES ARTS DE L'ONTARIO

Le Conseil des Arts | The Canada Council
du Canada | for the Arts

Printed in Canada

Dedicated to Betty Isabelle Emily Page, 1929–

I was born and the market fell.

Throughout *Crossing Arcs,* quotes from Betty Page
are set in italics and used with her permission.

Contents

I am lost, Mother

in the spaces you leave behind

    I cannot even see

        a shadow there to

            follow

            I have no way to comfort you in the

            empty room

            your mind now is

            doors and windows
            shut

            blinds hung
            closed

I don't think I have Alzheimer's. My memory is my own and I'm going to keep it.

Summerhouse

What We Don't Say

I snap off the radio.
She's coming downstairs.

"Why can't I stay?"
Picks up a tea towel and cup from the rack.
"I have nothing to go back for."

      – because already I'm worn out?
      – because when you're here
      I can do nothing else
      but answer your questions,
      find what you've lost,
      fix what you've broken,
      remember not to say,
      'I told you that before'
      – because watching you stumble
      down steps, over pebbles
      trips me over myself?

"Because there's too much to do.
No time for any fun."

She frowns at the counter,
slaps down her towel.

"Why does everyone think I can't
do anything anymore?

Don't tell me I'm useless!
Just tell me what to do and I'll do it," she says.

    – Just make the job:
    simple, easy.
    – Just provide:
    tools and supplies,
    old clothes she can get dirty,
    tea every hour.
    – Don't ask her to make decisions:
    'this colour or that?'
    – Don't step out of sight.
    – Don't leave her dangling,
    unsure what to do next.
    – Don't think out loud.
    – And when she tells you
    of the sketches
    she's made of the hayfield,
    don't say, 'you never did them'.

"Mom – please understand.
We want to spend a few weeks
together and alone."

          – Together? Alone? Alone like me? –
she doesn't say.

I drive her to the airport,
watch
as she's wheeled
up the ramp, through the gate,
to be flown back to her room,
the nurses,
the cleaning staff.

"Fuck!" I say to the lounge
full of travellers,
children.
"Sweet Mother of Jesus
fuck."

Summerhouse

My mother is with us
from the day we open the door
to mess and dirt and dust.
That first year, she brushes down spiders
the size of loonies, sweeps flies
from corners, washes rags
of curtains in buckets of well water,
scrubs birdshit from sills,
scrapes at paint and dirt,
pulls us through hardware stores
for nails, hooks, towel rods. Together,
we haul beds and dressers up the stairs.

And each night she argues
with my husband – all through the courses
of the meals he invents to match
her tastes and needs.
She has her own opinions
about how to fix the pump,
repair the beams,
tear down walls
and lay the new floor.

"My dad taught me how to
handle tools," she tells him.
Stands by with a broom
to knock him to safety
as he rewires the fusebox.
Shows him how to bang in nails
with three strong strokes –
"Shouldn't take more!"

"I can't take much more,"
he grumbles to me,
counting the days
till her train is due.

When I'm down east I feel a bond
– a reminiscence – of my grandma
and grandad being down there,
landing in Pictou, and then
Joggins, and Saint John.

Hanging Out to Dry

We plug in the brand new
roll-up washing machine,
hook it up to the sink,
like the one we had
when we were young.
Hang the clothes in the wind,
moving in matching arcs
around the whirlygig of lines
on the carousel pole.

She married so early
that our memories blend.
"Remember all the loads
we did in that old wringer?"

A sheet flaps, catches.
She ducks and laughs,
slaps it into place like a playful girl.
In our fifties and eighties
we've both been through the wash
enough times to fade
and wear every seam.

Paint stains and tears
meld with the cloth
of the overalls and teeshirts
we peg to the line.

Which are hers?
Which mine?

*To compare, use ratios. When you
were ten, I was three times your
age. Now it's eight to five. We get
closer as we get older.*

Clouding Over

Balancing the wine glass
on a book of poems,
pencil clutched between
middle and index finger,
along with cork screw, sunglasses,
Bartlett's quotations,
the lopsided apple
that fell on my head but
jarred nothing loose –

I make my way in
from the fading afternoon,
as insect-growing clouds
blow over the sun.

"There you are!" she greets me.
"Where did you go?
Why didn't you tell me?
You never tell me anything!"

It's like living in a fog. A drift.
Nowhere to touch down. I can't
get hold of anything.

A Waste of Time

"I'll do the dishes.
 At least that's something I can do."

She fills the sink with water
cool so her hands won't hurt.
Grease pools on the surface.
She won't rinse the plates.
A waste of time, she says,
time too precious
to spend on extra steps
when a horde of children called.

Forgets to wipe the counter.

And as often as I show her,
can't remember
where the cups are hung.

*This is stupid, being like this,
thoroughly annoys me. What's in
front of me is what I see.*

It Will Be Easy

I worry a lot about her dying
these days, not so much
about her, how she feels
or will feel
about her death.
I hope it will be easy,
simple as forgetting.
That she'll lie down one evening
and like the rain streaming over
the windows tonight,
just runnel away,
asleep
and snoring maybe
and then
not.

I'd give her this if I could, but still
I'm not worried about her.

If there's nothing, she may be
relieved to give way
to the sleep she always needed.

If there's a heaven, she'll be there,
though they may make her do the dishes.

If it's Nirvana, she'll be bored.
Set out to raise Cain.

*It's very frustrating. Sometimes
not even frustrating because
I can't remember what it's all
about. So then I don't worry about
it. Just look at what's happening
right here and right now.*

Before the Weather Turns

The second year, she starts
to strip a dressing table,
and when her hands begin to hurt,
hangs up hooks for cups and mugs,
puts up shelves for bowls.

Eats his good food and naps for hours.

And she talks. How she talks.
Every small disaster of the year behind,
every anxious moment still to come
runs past her lips as we work side by side.
Her arguments with the church,
frustration with the neighbours,
opinions on the news.

When the wind begins to blow
September cool,
she joins me in a race to paint
the sills and frames
before the weather turns.
My husband scrapes ahead.
Can hardly keep up.

We always did talk a lot, the whole fan damily. Even our arguments were eloquent.

Stubborn as an old horse,
she's out every morning
before I'm awake
in work gloves and sweats,
blue hat pulled down,
hair tussling with the wind,
paintbrush aloft.
Refuses to come in
even when the breeze
starts to dribble and spit.

The neighbours laugh and tease her:
"They're working you to death!"

"No longer than a week
next year,"
he says to me.

Crossing Arcs

"Don't be ridiculous,
it's far too big for me."

I hold the bathing suit
up to my chest
and see she's right.

Somehow we've slipped
along crossing arcs
as I curve into middle age,
she slides into old.

I pull the suit on.
Have to yank and pull.

The one I've given her
gapes at the legs,
sags at the waist.

In the water, I pause as we
splash through the shallows.
Reach for her hand.

*It's a good time to write poems
about this, because there are so
many old people around. It'll give
them a feeling that they're not
alone.*

Wood Filler

The third year, she buys putty
and paint and wood filler.
"I meant to fix the sills last year,
I'll do them now."

I ask her to help hang new blinds,
get the hardware,
look for the electric drill.

But she won't wait,
Tries to screw into the old wood,
till her arthritic fingers buckle.
"Why do we need new holes anyway,
the old ones are fine!'

I put on the tea.
"Let's do it later," I say.

The sills are still unpainted.
The filler on the shelf.

The new blinds open and close
on supports she doesn't see.

Revelations

"And what's your revelation this time?" I ask,
as we settle with our first, our endless cup of tea,
sit back to watch the clouds chase the tide down the bay.

It's an old game of ours. I'm eager to hear,
after months apart, about her projects and plans –
always a surprise, always a new start.

"Oh nothing much," she says. "Did I tell
you what the painting teacher said . . . ?"

The story is from last year.
I've heard it a dozen times.

"Did you bring your paints with you?"

"No . . . not this trip . . . but . . .
I'm going to start painting again . . .
did I tell you . . ."

It doesn't make sense.

She must be just beyond a door,
or a tree, or the crest of a hill.
Somewhere she can't hear me.

These trailing threads of words
that loop back into themselves
or fray into a question –
this is not my mother.

It's some kind of joke,
some masquerade.

I don't think it's funny,
I don't want to play.

So I did skid to a stop. I remember
feeling the same frustration with
the whole thing, the idiocy.

Eleven Lines

She tells me the sky is a watercolour,
shows us eleven lines of colour in the sea.

My husband searches for paints,
comes home with felt pens,
all he could find in the country store.

The pens won't do,
though she watches them sideways
for days, before she says –

"It was nice of him to buy them,
but put them away.

If only I could stop seeing..."

Hay Bales

The meadow beyond the window
changes day by day. From high grass,
to first mowing, to raking, to bales.

I could paint that, she says.

Each day, tells me how
she would layer the scene
in greens and yellows and greys.

On the last day of her visit,
she dwells on every bale,
describes each shadow,
how it turns with the sun.

I do not lift the paper,
from the bookshelf nearby,
the pencils and felt pens
that have waited every day.

She does not ask.

*If only my mind didn't fill with
pictures – the colours, the layers –
then I could let it go.*

It Closes like a Heart

Her words are all questions now:
"When am I leaving?
Who's going to meet me?
What was I doing?
I was working on something."

Everything she starts
she drops halfway through.

In the last few days,
I nudge her toward the dresser
she began the first year.
She settles with her rags and cans,
wipes off the old paint
as gently as if the swirled wood
underneath were skin.

"Look, look at this.
Look how the wood
is cut to match the panels
across the front of the drawers.
How beautiful it is.
It closes like a heart."

That night, she stays up
to finish the final sanding.
We roll the dresser back,
ready for next year
when she says she'll rub it
with three coats of oil.

"Where are we going?"
she asks yet again
as we head towards home.

And he answers her again.
As we drive down the highway,
he answers her in detail
again and again
and again.

It's living in the now – it's a pocket memory. I know I'm here because you're here.

Fixing Splits

This scraping and repainting of split wood shingles
is tedious, messy – work that doesn't end.

And though I dream my way through websites and flyers
of cement-fibre wall shingles (that never need painting),

red cedar window frames – that never need painting –
wood-composite railings that never need painting!

what we actually do is spend our days up a ladder
scraping patch by patch. Filling splits and breaks.

Just a small, white house in a hayfield on a bay.
With a neighbour who lends tools.

Friends who drop by to see what she's doing
this windy afternoon.

We went down again years later,
went to visit the neighbours.
Of course they were still there.

Learning to Forget

The fourth year, she returns
to the half-done dressing table.
Rinses the dishes, leaves them for me
to put away on the shelves.
Waves to the neighbours.
Cheerfully says, "I don't remember."
Greets me as my sister,
laughs when she finds I'm me.

They said this would happen,
the friends who console us –
a short, happy state
when she would stop fighting,
learn how to forget.

In between, there are hours
when we talk as we used to.
Neither of us hears
me repeat names and facts
over and over
and over.

Fighting the Trap

The mouse fights the trap
for almost half an hour
under the rain-smacked roof.
We lie awake, our fingers
quaking with its quakes,
its rattles against the rafter.
We lie and will it dead,
as it struggles, voiceless,
the pauses between rattles
countable by breaths
held longer
and longer –
then –
just as we hope,
again it drags the trap
through the crate of the ceiling.

Forces us out of bed.

I huddle by the fire
as my husband climbs on a chair,
opens the hatch to attic,

gloves and flashlight
and two-by-four in hand
while the mouse scrabbles louder.

Whacks it quiet.
throws it out the door.

But just look out. Watch me.
That's what's got me through all
the major crises of my life is my
anger. And I refuse to feel guilty
about it.

Refusing the Bait

Suddenly, over a supper
of haddock and greens.

"Why won't you let me finish what I'm saying?"
she snaps at him.
"You act like I'm stupid and old.

"And you – you never listen!"
Why are you always telling me what to do?
I can look after myself!"

I'm stuck, fork in air,
mushroom dripping sauce.

"Of course you can," he says.
"You tell her off. Your daughter's
always been bossy."

The arguments they've had
for so many years
about science and religion
and politics and art
are done. He no longer
leaps into the fray.

Refuses any bait.
Speaks as he does
to me, when I cry.

"I don't want to go back,"
she says to him then.

"Don't worry," he tells her.
"Stay as long as you want.
You don't have to leave.
There's no rush at all."

Sometimes I feel like a spent
volcano.

Arguing with the Tide

I sit on the rock as the tide pours in,
white-lipped, turbulent,
imagine ways to keep my mother safe
from myself and all the champions
who want to run her life.
Imagine the accusations, confusions,
misunderstandings, if her children fight,
mother caught in the middle.
Who to believe, who could be wrong?

A daylight nightmare
as the water rushes and sucks
into deadly undercurrents
where the river meets the bay
over mud that looks safe
but can pull you in to your chest
with one misstep.
Lush green eel-grass and sandpaper rock
offer no holds for a swimmer
caught in the pull.
Each year, someone drowns.

*I had to get angry. There's anger
and fear, one or the other, and I
choose anger. Anger is what keeps
you alive.*

Waves scrape and growl,
break against my knees,
chase me from the shore
up the slope to the hayfield,
through Queen Anne's Lace,
thistle and vetch.

Later tonight
the tide will back out
a full flat mile, the far-off edge
not even a murmur beyond splinters
of moonlight on stones and sand –

       large flat stones, firm plates of sand
       where I can walk
       for a few hours' ebb.

Self-Portrait in Black and White

I glue it in the scrapbook I've made
to remind her of her artworks –

a high-contrast copy of a pencil sketch
she did years ago.

Main lines still in place, proportions correct,
but delicacy, rounding

smudged into white. Erratic dashes
of expression remain

around mouth and eyes, in lines too
sharp, too coarsely edged.

Art
reduced to caricature.

Leaving Summer Behind

We drive away from summer through two days of trees,
trees and mud, mud and trees in a dull repeat –
bare racks on hard scrabble against a metal sky,
scriven by pepper toss of starlings, jag of geese,
hunch of raven on stump and dead tip. Each field
shakes gulls into the air, crows rankle in ditches,
hawks drop so fast towards rodents in the straw
they seem to leave contrails etched on the grey.

"Every year they build nests. All those birds."
I thought she was asleep, dozing in the back
on the pillows and bags. "Thousands and thousands
of nests. By spring, the trees will all be empty again.
What happens to nests when the winter comes?"

Where did it go, that painting of
the woods – with the ochre trees?
Did I give it away?

Let's see what happens this winter.
It'll certainly be abstract.
It'll have to be beyond realism.

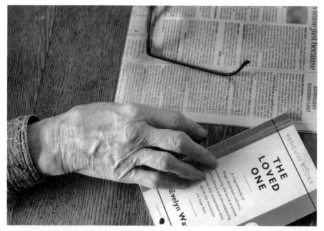

Residence

Survival

"I'm going to move to a retirement home.
I've had enough."

We've been mentioning the idea
for months – showing her ads –
but it's she who decides, her own decision,
made all in one day.

I made the choice because no-one else could.

"Right now. I don't want to ever carry bags
up steps again. Take out the garbage.
Shovel snow from the walk.
I don't want to cook even one more meal."

She doesn't have to think about it.
Something inside, some careful wary beast
watches all the time.

Watches out for itself.
For her, its lair.

Answering Machine

"Clear out the apartment.
Give it all away."

Weeks and weeks of work
for my sister and her husband,
for me and mine,
who move what we can
to her twelve by twenty room,
pack the rest into boxes
to await a second look,
a cooler mood.

As we sort and dismantle
I tell myself she'll never again
cook a pot of stew
and invite us to share,
never amble through the park
from her place to ours,
never fight with the landlord,
sing with the neighbours.

But I can't make it real.

It clicks in the day
I listen to her message
on the new machine.

Hear her voice hesitate. Stumble
over words.

*It's very confusing and unsettling
but I'm determined not to let it
drive me nuts. I won't give up. It's
self defence.*

Hands

She takes off her boots.
Coat still buttoned,
turns from the hall
into the apartment
she left a week before.
One final trip to pick up
final things.

Steps through the arch
into the living room.

Her hands come together.
Fold around each other
as if against cold.

The couch is gone.
Her lamp.
Her chair.
The floor a mess
of movers' tracks.

A few more steps.

She stops.
Bends her head
into my shoulder.

I put my arms around her –

her hands, between us,
still closed around something
no-one can hold.

*Acceptance and loss. Holding on
to life and what it was.*

True Reckoning

This wandering, where she hits
the walls of her room –
north not where it should be,
sun gone from windows
that used to be filled.

Her square's moved sideways
and halfway around.
How can I turn this space
to face into summer –
towards the homes she knew,
where north was straight ahead,
east was the morning,
west the afternoon,
and south what held
when all else dimmed?

In February shade
as I close the door behind me,
I know I leave her askew,
triangulated into a corner
at the back of a crooked building
that can't be understood

skidding out of control
as the map folds up
to a darkened point.

What does it feel like? Pods.
Skyhooks. Parachutes suspended
between sky and earth. Like I'm
in a space station detached from
everything and all the memories
are little threads trying to bring
me back.

Visitors

The rest of us cope
in our different ways.
Two of us in town.
Four spread across the continent
sending advice
about exercise, running shoes,
potassium, sudoku.
Some call every week,
all visit when they can –
visits planned
without her involvement
for the very first time.
No longer will they sleep
on a mattress on her floor,
no longer rise late
to drink tea and talk
for a whole, unplanned day.

From now on, they'll stay
with my sister or me.
Make forays to see her
for an hour. Or two.

*When they come, I'll take them out
for dinner, take them out to the
rowdiest pub I can find!*

Diagnosis

"Have I had a stroke?
Is that what happened to me?"

"It's Alzheimer's, Mom."

"Did I know that?
Did you tell me?"

"Yes, we went to the doctor.
Do you remember what he said?"

"No, I don't remember.
I'm losing my memory, you know.
It's very annoying. Makes me furious!

"But I'm going to beat it.
I'm not going to give in.
I'm getting better every day."

I smooth her hair.
She used to push me off.

"Did I have a stroke?
What's happened to me?"

Orienteering

She's figured it out
with her Girl Guide compass.
Where the doors go,
how the walls fit.
Marked her table
with a line pointing north.

She's met the man down the hall
who calls if she doesn't appear
for breakfast or lunch,
meets her downstairs for a walk by the river.
Serves her Scotch in a tiny glass.

His name is Bill.
They play billiards together.
Name and game together
easier to remember.

"Sometimes I give him
a hug. That's all.
None of that other stuff.
I think he misses his wife.
She's not long gone."

One day, they start singing
in the Bistro, against the rules,
and everyone joins in.

Now the "I-Can't-Singers"
meet every week
wherever they choose.

*"A lot of the stuff that's come and gone
is gone, and what you're left with is
what you basically are."*

Tomorrow. Right Now.

Lunch. Tea. Each moment flows along
with its own completion,
at its own pace.

"I'll start the singing group
as soon as the snow flies."

But there are places to go –
Upstairs to see a friend.
To the lounge to play pool.

"The concert sounds good.
I'll phone for tickets."

Tomorrow. Right now it's
time for a short nap.
Then downstairs to tea.

"That drawing needs reframing.
I'll do it next week."

The actions she describes
are sensible, fit the context.

Live in a friendly space.

The space of a phone call,
the space of now.

*I'm an animated film without a
story.*

Looking behind the Words

Crosswords and cyberquotes
consume her mornings.
Mornings too hungry without that meal.
Small leaps, small successes
are snacks and sustenance
against the hollow
that sucks the words away.

She looks up. "Hi –
What could this be –
nine letters – begins
and ends with 't'.
Boisterous, overbearing,
a virago, a shrew – "

"Termagant?" I ask.
She grins. "That's me."

So they finally put a fancy
name onto something that we
considered to be just getting old.
Nuts to this. My mind is not going
to play games with me. Who does
it think it is?

Skeletoning Down

What use is a label?
This season "Type 2,"
next "OCD" or "Alzheimer's" –
all glowers to fill a garden
of named despair.

No animal would bother.
A dog struck by sugar shock
simply lies down,
a cat with a growing cancer
creeps away mute.

Words birth guilt –
blame – remorse –

when all this really is
is one way to fall,
leaf among leaves
skeletoning
down.

Letter to Myself : Learn

Don't bother to deny it.
Your brain is going.
Breaking down.
You must simplify.
Drive into every sponge
of remaining grey tissue
the same repeated patterns,
so even as they fail,
one by one,
you still may be able
to hold on to a few.

In this state, choose well.

Judge by your mother.

Learn. Learn.

And that covers four generations.
I think it's kind of hereditary, so
watch out.

Like a Baby, or a Child

The hangover clenched
on my lids and between my brows
tranforms as I sleep into an anxious
dream of my mother rousing me
with a cooling cup of tea
that keeps slipping in her hands
as she bends into my drowsing,
bends for a kiss,
though I turn my head away.

As dreams do, the scene shifts
to racks of baby clothes
where I'm searching for a gift
for my daughter's first child.
Under cover of helping,
my mother leans towards me,
whispers "Move me,
like a baby, or a child,
to wherever you are – "

As I wake, we
both weep.

Losing the Tools

This time it's forks and spoons
and bottles of glue
that keep me awake.
What will she be
to herself
without her tools –
she who always knew
how to replace a washer
change a fuse, fix a chair?
Or without her favourite cup?

I walk in the door
of her full-service suite
and she greets me with "Tea!"
as she always did,
but she doesn't have a pot
or kettle in her room,
and the dining hall downstairs
uses china so fine
each cup holds no more
than half of what she wants.

But it's okay. And I think it was
right. When I look back at my
grandma and my mom, they did
the same thing. And I think, if they
can, I can.

I can't take it in.
All of the things
that marked her as her
by what she could do –
stored, or given away.

A bare two decades
separate our lives.
What will my daughters
choose, for me,
to leave on the shelf?

Fire Needs

"Air –
distance –
closeness –
fuel – "

She crouches on the bench
by my fireplace, piling logs,
stuffing in newspaper
to produce the perfect flame.

"My father taught me how."
As she's taught me,
and I, my girls.

No fires in her building.
Someone might get hurt.

"If you know how to light a fire,
you've always got warmth."

Someone might, but not by her.

She lifts the heavy poker,
the awkward shovel,
wedges them together
to shift a stuck log.

Her practised hands
exact.

*I don't want to be treated as if
I've got some horrible disease.
Because, if so, everyone's going
to get it sooner or later. I can be
smug about that!*

Time to Plan

After coming here, she doesn't need
to worry anymore about
meals, medicine, safety.
There are people to talk to,
complaints to make.

"Now I'm regaining
my spirits and health,
now is the time to plan
my next ten years.

"Another cup of tea? "
She's bought a pot and kettle
from the hardware down the street.

"Maybe I'll take a cruise,
just keep changing ships.

"Or move to Nova Scotia.
I could live there all winter,
get it ready for you in spring.

If I must live husked like a nut,
dammit you'll hear me rattle and
shake in my shell!

"I could do the Elder Hostels,
enrol in art school.

"Go back to the Anglican church.
Good music. Church suppers.

"Or visit each of my six children,
two months each year.

"I've never really had the chance
 to do all I meant to do."

We talk, and talk,
and talk.

Apology

I tell these stories,
look at her from outside
judging, judging,
hold her up to the cold grey light
of pixellating fact to
evaluate, analyse, label
what she is, make notes
on her life closing in,
on her brain lobes shrivelling,
on confusion tying her tighter
and tighter into its tangle,
keyboard the details
(gossip disguised as love)
of her intimate decay.
How can I imagine this is
in any way alright or that I will
ever be forgiven
for presuming to describe
as if it were truth
what is happening behind her eyes –
where I, full of orders, can
not go?

February Cold

"I want to go home," she tells me
today, and starts to cry.
My mother,
who never does.

"But there's no home to go to,
is there?" she says,
when she sees my face.

"And this is my home.
The things I've crammed in.
The single bed."

I've brought her silk cushions
to put at its head.
And a box of chocolates,
the special kind,
which she shouldn't have.

"Did I tell you Bill's gone?"

It's Valentine's Day.

*Now I should think of all the lovers
I've had. It would probably shock
the children.*

Art Class

At noon, I call, and she wakes to the phone's
first panic ring. "Just got up . . .",
her tongue still stuck to night,
who finished a dozen tasks
before the day began.

By the time I arrive,
she's searching for brushes and paint.

One picture on her wall
is stepping slow to its polished end.
A band of blue one week.
The next, a swath of green.

We talk of where the waves
will go on the blocked-in sea.
The angle of sun on sand.

A sleeping scene, wakened each week
for a half-hour burst of energy.

*Like this painting, my life includes
all kinds of things. A bit of this
and a bit of that. Like a palette.
Personal colours. That's blue –
that's where I start.*

"Always thought the time would come,"
she says, "when I had time."
And now it has.
And now she does.

To sleep. To fiddle with what's left over
from the busy years.

"No rush," she tells me. "This time,
I intend to get it right."

I know what it's like from inside,
but not what it looks like from outside.

This Is Now

I Am Imagining Myself Old

I am imagining myself old
because she's not what she was.
I haul my five decades hand by hand up the stairs,
listen anxiously to my heart beat,
shy away from salt, spices, sugar, wine,
lie late into the day, wondering how many
more I have left.

This is not what she does.
Faced by clear decay
in a diminished, sunless space,
she covers the walls with her paintings,
the shelves with her pottery and books,
grabs every bit of life that blunders her way.

"My grandmother lived to a hundred and three."

This is not true, but what use are facts?

This is now. As I said, what else can I do?

The Good Years

Thirty years married, thirty divorced,
Still they shadow step.

"How is he," she asks me, "and his wife?
I'm so glad she's there to look after him.
She'll keep him in line!"

"How's she doing?" he wants to know.
"Do you think I should drop by
next time I come to town?"

His eyesight is fading
as fast as her memory.

They're both writing histories
of the good years.

I may be losing my memory, but it's a discriminating memory. I have things you will never know – no matter what I remember or forget. There are places in my mind where you can never go.

Sign of Respect

Afraid she's fallen or had a stroke
when she doesn't answer my knock,
I have the nurse unlock her door,
ignoring with a daughter's disdain
the clearly written post-it –
"Do Not Disturb"
in her school-teacher hand –
stuck above the knob,
and can only laugh
with surprise and a kind of
relief and delight
to see two bare bodies
half rise on the bed,
as I step in.

"Sorry! – " I back out fast.

Who gave me the right
to breach a shut door?
What made me sure
age had smothered that flame?

All her lovers.
I'll remember.

Wrist Cuff

"You're dead, you know," the doctor said,
when he read the numbers back.

I think of that each time
I strap the bracelet on
to check my blood pressure
morning, noon, night,
at his command.
Each time it's higher
no matter how I slow my breath,
slump in my chair,
think calm thoughts.

The cuff itself is confused
by what it finds, soars beyond sense,
starts the puff again,
tumbles into "err"
before marking, replaced,
how day after day the readings climb.

Tonight I prop my wrist
on *Alzheimer's for Dummies*,

which, for all its good advice,
doesn't ease my grief.
Doesn't help me help my mother
to be herself again.
Doesn't help me answer friends
with impossible, hopeful news.

Buzz, buzz again.
Constrict. Release.
The mechanical sigh.

Fingers shock
as blood returns.

*Free-floating anxiety – it runs in
the family. I could always find
something to worry about. Now I
don't have to worry any more.*

Her Mother's Cheeks

"You have my mother's cheeks,"
she says, and pinches one.
"You look so much like her.
Now that you've put on some –
you know – a little weight.
Those rosy cheeks like hers,
tucked up under blue eyes."

And yes, I do
mother her.
Yes, I tuck her in
and lay an extra blanket
on the end of the bed.

And yes, perhaps, one day
she may call me mother.

How will I respond?

*Now I understand what my
mother was going through. I
thought she was just being lazy
and slow. And she was so good
to me . . .*

One good thing – I love reading. I read a book a day. And then I finish the book and close it, and say to myself, I wonder what that was all about? So I read it again. Means I can read every book five times.

Comfort

The novels I read
close comfort around me.

The poems I write
scratch trails through my gut

like a cat who's swallowed
a thread of wire

and tries to tooth it out.
Incomprehensible pains

that even when they pass
leave cramps as a mark.

"Isn't that what poetry
is supposed to do:
to enlighten, to point out,
to sharpen perception?"

This is a failing mind?

In my room and hers
books cover the floor.

Walled Out of Sight

What you notice when you're sick is how
you don't want to ask your husband –
who just drove to the store for crackers,
and went downstairs twice for soda
and to the bathroom for the thermometer –

you don't want to ask him
to search the sewing basket
for a certain kind of needle
to sew up the sweater you're knitting.

So you smile and nod and say nothing
till you fall asleep in your chair,
and he lifts the wool from your hands,
tangling the skein.

What does she need, but doesn't want
to bother me about,
mother smiling and nodding
from across the room?

What's walled out of sight
behind her careful calm?

*Sometimes I think, why can't
I just take a pill and forget all
this? Nothing more I can do or
say or change. And then I go and
rearrange the flowers, and have a
cup of tea . . .*

Letter to Myself

If this happens to me
I will kill myself.
I don't mean to let the words out.
And with my daughters
manage to refrain.
But to him, they slip out suddenly
through cracks in conversation,
at stopped moments in halls.
Nights, I plan the method
that will cause least pain.
Look most like an accident.
Google has thousands of recipes
but not one is certain.
Not Scotch and pills and winter:
they say you vomit it up.
Not slipping through a hole in ice:
someone is always watching.
And which backyard, which lake
will I choose to forever poison
for those left behind?
There will be no more words.
Not even, I'm not sorry.

Colouring the Dragon

"Look how the lines twist –
is that a foot or a mouth,
a bit of wing or sky?"

Colouring books of Chinese dragons,
Celtic knots, monsters and saints
from the Book of Kells
engross her for hours.

"It's fascinating. A puzzle.
And the colours. Did you give them to me,
all these pens? Look at the fluorescent yellow –
how it makes the other colours
spring from the page."

"They were a gift from your friend –
eighty markers for your eightieth birthday.
You remember her, you've known her
for twenty-five years."

My health is fine. I'm as healthy as a pig in rut. Just let me get a man. Too bad most of them here are old . . .

"I should send the finished pages
to all my children. Refrigerator art!
Or they can hang them in windows
so the light shines through.
That's your Great Grandma, they can say,
that fluorescent yellow dragon
with the green and purple spikes!

The pens are running out –
I need to replace them. Where
did I get them? I can't
create anymore."

As My Mother Searches for Love

As my mother searches for love
I am cutting free from sex.
It doesn't draw me anymore.
Nothing much does
as the end of it all looms nearer,
as I say to myself and everyone
that I've never had so much time,
never been more happy
than I am now – an ambiguous
statement if you turn it around.
True, though, this retirement
offers time and more
to worry, time and more to drive
through slippery winter snows,
bring her home for an evening
of fire and food and talk,
time and more to calculate
the remaining months or years,
the factors that might change
her cheerful surface that fools so many,

who look at me – 'why are you saying
she's gone when she's clearly here?
Clearly here and whole?'
And oh, I wish it were so.

*It's so important to see you – to
keep my sanity, literally, to keep
in touch with reality. Otherwise it
would be very easy to get spaced
out in a place like this, to wonder
what you were doing here.*

Black Day

How would I last without my house,
without the glimpse of river
as I turn down the street,
without the bustle of finches
and chickadees round the porch
where we sit and eat our dinner,
call out to neighbours
from behind the screen of grapevines,
or without our evening walk in the park,
where children bring bread for the ducks,
dogs and owners romp unleashed,
herons flap, blackbirds preen,
and irises unfurl.

In a room like hers, sealed from the earth,
looking out on a parking lot,
how could I find a path
through a black day
with no fireplace to burn
these useless scraps of words?

Without the scent of ferns?

*I've got my pictures and my couch.
Everything has a story. I remember
that couch in the window of the
secondhand store – it glowed
orange and gold. And that little
table. I glued it together, redid a
whole panel . This is what's left.
And it's not bad.*

Having Grieved Enough for Now

What does it mean?
Is it just a bad joke?
I hold all that's happened
up to my eyes
as if it were jumbled
in child's kaleidoscope,
turn the tube through tumbles
of yellow, red, blue –
shards and slivers and fragments
in a cracked cascade
that clink into place
after place
after place
with a small glass hiss.

Why her? Why this?
I turn and turn.

Each burst is different.
Each unrelated to the one before.

A Society of Friends

"Who will watch over the closing
minds of our elders?"

Did she make this up?
A quote from a Quaker text
that sounds so familiar
I'm sure I've read it somewhere.

The elders in our Meeting
were kind-voiced, wry.
My mother, I assumed,
would become one too,
as I would follow.

All those years of worship,
activism, action,
teaching, committees –

And now she is lost.
Can no longer sit
through the unbroken silence
of Meeting for Worship.
Is afraid of tears.

Of greetings
from friends
she no longer knows.

Who am I to God, and he to
me? I had to leave. God was too
powerful there, in the silence. Too
much to handle.

From across the Bay

I wake up, and my mother
is in my mind full bloom,
silver hair sculpted
and bouncy as a boy's cowlick,
eyes blue as the sky
unscissoring from the clouds,
she is quick-stepping forward
in her red shirt and overalls,
the solid bones and flesh
of her fingers warm and dry
around mine –
        or so I think
for a moment, in bed,
before opening my eyes.

I think my husband, by my side,
is her. Turn over,
pull the quilt across his shoulders.

"Are you warm enough?" I ask.

Deep memories, compartments
of memories that spring to mind.
The words unlock them.

Expecting her to answer.
Expecting to hear her voice
as clear and singing as a bell across the bay –

"Fine, I'm fine.
I have plans for the day – this gorgeous sunny day.

How are you, this morning?
What will you do?"

How the Earth Lets Go

The thought of her
closing down
makes me stare out
into a shivery April dusk
at crusts of grey snow
still heaped on lawns
like disintegrating bread,
watch how they dribble apart,
collapse into the ground
chunk by soggy chunk,
dropping leaves and mud and dust
as the piles and slices of ice
lose their structure,
round at the corners,
soak the earth below.

Fill it
with cold.

This is not reality, my reality.
This is where you go when you're
finished.

Conundrums

Which is worse?

To lose your sight
or your mind.

To be safe and smothered
or alone and slipping.

Where would you rather be?

Far away and worried
or close and overloaded.

In the middle
or at the edge.

Angry
or afraid.

Rushes Her Down

And yet, she's still here.
Still behind the windows
lit by gas lamps and firelight,
still leading the beat
in family songs,
still at the centre
pumping on the guitar
with her laugh-tooled skin
and quartz-blue eyes
and hair like a silver mop,
still here, as she burnishes
from grey to glow
and her words fly away like
flickers, gulls
tossing in wind –
memories spray and tangle like
ribbons of mist
steaming from the bay –
thoughts come and go like
flames in the stove, like
the wiver of a candle, like
the breath that blows back
into the crowded room

as I slip away
into salt and damp,
into darkness by the shore.

Look back through the glass.
Look back
as my mother,
small and gold,
slips into my hands

        and I close my palms
        around her,
        hold her
        as the current
                rushes her down.

What I put in at the end is the window,
as if you could get through
to the other side.

Betty Page: A Sketch

The oldest of three children, Betty Isabelle Emily Page was born in 1929 in Roselands, a small suburban neighbourhood now incorporated into the city of Toronto. Subject to an ear infection at age two, in the era before antibiotics, she spent much of the next seven years in hospital. When home, she enjoyed taking her little brother and his friends from the neighbourhood on outdoor expeditions. On fishing trips with her father, she would paint watercolours of the woods, and went on to paint pictures in autograph books for her friends, and sell postcard-sized paintings as birthday and Christmas presents for a quarter. She later attended the now-famous Saturday morning art classes organized by Arthur Lismer at the Art Gallery of Toronto (now the Art Gallery of Ontario).

When her father died in her teens, Betty completed high school, placing top in her class, and received a scholarship to attend Normal School in Toronto in 1948–49. There she met her future husband, Gordon George McClure, who had been born on the same day of the same year in Toronto, and had also attended AGT art classes. They married that January, both aged nineteen, and after graduation taught at country schools and in Toronto, and had four children.

In 1956 they moved the family to Ottawa, where Gordon worked for the Ottawa Board of Education and started the first class for disturbed children in Ontario. They were both instrumental in strengthening the Ottawa Meeting of the Religious Society of Friends (Quakers), and quickly became active in Ottawa's growing cultural community and left-wing and pacifist political groups.

By 1960, they had six children, Susan, Peter, Andrew, Mary, Martha, and Ann. A few years later Betty returned to full-time teaching, eventually concentrating on developing innovative music and reading programs for slow learners; the music program became a provincially accredited high school course. She somehow found time to study art and produce several hundred oil paintings and drawings, many of which sold informally and at art shows to friends and admirers of her work; to teach art classes for the city; and to produce hundreds of pottery pieces, which she sold at craft shows, for example on the terrace at the National Arts Centre. She completed a Bachelor of Arts in Sociology through the Carleton University extension program, graduating the same year as her daughter Mary.

The marriage ended after thirty years, and Betty retired from teaching soon after, in part to concentrate on her painting. She moved to Toronto for several years to join family, and came back to Ottawa in the 1990s. In the next decade Betty had two solo art shows, one of paintings and one of drawings, both almost entirely sold out. She also worked with Susan for more than a year on the millennial project *Convergence: Poems for Peace*, herself producing 2500 art prints and supervising the production by artists across Canada of 1000 more artworks, used to wrap poems for Parliamentarians and for distribution nation-wide.

Betty fulfilled two long-time dreams in the 1990s by building a cottage in Quebec and buying a small house in Mechanicsville in Ottawa. She sold the latter when living there became too difficult, and moved twice before settling into the retirement residence where she now lives. Before the move, she was diagnosed with very early stage Alzheimer's disease, and has since lost much of her short-term memory. She continues to live independently in her own studio apartment, and to engage in many activities, including leading a singing group and participating in a study of memory disorders. Betty recently turned eighty, and is the matriarch of a family of six children and spouses, fifteen grandchildren, and, at latest count, five great-grandchildren. Long life runs in the family, and she is currently planning her next twenty years.

Afterword

I began writing these poems when I first became aware of a change in my mother's relationship with the world. That was about seven years ago. Since then, she has been diagnosed with Alzheimer's Disease, and has moved to a retirement residence. As I write this, her short-term memory has almost completely disappeared. The first section of the book is set at our summer house on the Bay of Fundy, during my mother's annual visits. The second covers her voluntary move from an apartment to a retirement residence during the same period in Ottawa. The third widens to include a variety of voices and places, and focuses on my own growing understanding of the implications of my mother's situation for me.

When Marty Gervais, of Black Moss press, offered to publish the poems as a book, I realized I didn't want them to go out into the world without my mother's permission and blessing, and her voice. For the first, her reaction to publication – repeated many times over the next several months – was "Great, there are so many people with memory problems – they'll be interested. Go ahead." For the second, I began reading the poems to her, and noting down her reactions and comments. With Betty's permission, I have included a number of these responses, as well as some of her more general comments, throughout the book.

My warm thanks to the many people who have accompanied my mother and me on this journey. The book draws on sonata form for its structure; I am grateful to my brother Andrew McClure for exploring this with me.

The photographs of my mother and myself were taken by photographer, poet, and publisher Marty Gervais in November 2008 and April 2009, and are used with her permission. They add immeasurably to the book, as does his sensitive editing of the text. Book artist Karen Monck has again done an outstanding job of imaginative design.

My special thanks to my father Gordon and stepmom Anne and my siblings Ann, Martha, Mary, Andrew, and Peter for their support of this project. I would particularly like to thank my sister Mary McClure for her care of our mother. Many writing friends have also given much appreciated help through their intelligent reading of an unusual manuscript, notably Ronnie R. Brown (who suggested the book's title), Betsy Struthers, Colin Morton, and Renate Mohr. As always, my husband Ian and our daughters Morel and Aven and son-in-law Mark, along with many friends, have offered encouragement and advice.

My admiration and warmest thanks go to my mother, Betty Page, whose courage, optimism, and enthusiasm for life will continue to guide me through what may be a darkening time. I hope these poems shed some light and offer some comfort for others on the same journey.

Susan McMaster
Minasville, Nova Scotia
1 June 2009

Every book has to have something sad. Without that, it's a fairy tale.
People of my age have been through two wars, a depression,
epidemics – we can handle anything.